THE MEASURE OF THE YEAR

GAEL SELLWOOD

Published in Great Britain in 2018
by Mascot Media, Norfolk, UK.
Email: mascot_media@btinternet.com
www.mascotmedia.co.uk

© 2018 Mascot Media Ltd

A CIP catalogue record for this book is
available from the British Library.

ISBN: 978-1-9998457-8-0

Written by Gael Sellwood.
Designed by Alan Marshall.
Edited by Marion Scott Marshall.

Printed by Swallowtail Print, Drayton Industrial Park,
Taverham Road, Drayton, Norwich, Norfolk NR8 6RL.
Email: contact@swallowtailprint.co.uk
www.swallowtailprint.co.uk

ALL PHOTOGRAPHS © RACHEL WARNE (WWW.RACHELWARNE.CO.UK)

*The Rose and the
Woodpecker (detail)*

DEDICATION
*'The Measure of the Year' is
dedicated to my dear, kind
and supportive husband of
30 years, Michael, without
whose love and support I would
achieve very little: thank you,
my darling, and to our beloved
cocker spaniels Hope and Ruby.
You all mean the world to me.*

A GARDEN TO CHERISH

The setting sold the property; the garden sold the house; and it was the red-berried holly that sold the garden. The cottage sits in the middle of one half of the plot, which measures three-and-a-half acres and is bisected by a shingle drive.

As we approached slowly, we looked with curiosity either side of the drive. This was a place that we had passed on innumerable occasions. There was no need for us to drive along the lane, but we did. The location opposite the church seemed special; a place for contemplation and reflection. That this very place was now obtainable seemed beyond belief.

On the left of the drive were dark rhododendrons and holly trees – several of them laden with berries and seemingly the only bright thing on a very cold, damp November day. Also on the left was a dark,

dark hedge over which we could not see. The memory of the laden holly trees still sends a frisson of excitement through me. I had no expectations of the cottage; the holly tree was enough.

In the event, the cottage (which dates from 1640) has provided a perfect home in which an artist can thrive, surrounded by a garden and landscape of dreams. The cottage used to belong to the 'Bury', the large house across the lane. In the 1920s it was sold to a retired army major. He set about making modest alterations to the cottage and somewhat more ambitious changes to the garden – building on the foundations and structure that already existed. Significantly, he added to the box (*Buxus sempervirens*) structures in the form of large balls, planted hedging, and supposedly dug out several feet of soil into which he placed an ericaceous peaty soil

– later planted with rhododendrons and azaleas. When we took it on the garden had retained this structure, and we worked with an experienced designer to add to and enrich the existing garden, rather than seeking to make our mark. The garden has a certain faded grandeur to it, giving a clue to its art deco origins. Circles, curves and balls all provide their playful and decorative part, adding to the chocolate box prettiness.

This was a garden to cherish and enjoy, to enhance rather than to make our own. We are simply the custodians of the house and its land; merely passing through.

The holly continues to thrive, when it isn't being nibbled by deer, but there is plenty to go around. It has long been a favoured subject for paintings; the association with the first magical encounter is very strong indeed.

Holly and ribbon

A POCKETFUL OF TREASURES

Hedgerow flowers

My fascination with holly, texture, colour and form started long before my relationship with the house and gardens pictured on the preceding pages. This artist's story is no doubt similar to many others and yet, at the same time, very different.

At school I studied art, biology, history and Latin. I was always most comfortable in the biology lab and art room – creating scientific drawings of broad bean seedlings, pin-eyed and thrum-eyed primroses and more, as shown in Maud Jepson's beautifully drawn school textbook, originally published in 1938, and still used in the 1970s and early 1980s. The gathering of plant material and its analysis and description was always a balm in an otherwise competitive world. Essentially precise, reflective and analytical, this exercise in observation and drawing was an escape. The rich outer world made for a rich inner world where colours and textures became all powerful, making me feel omniscient.

Yet, it wasn't until many years later that I fully made sense of these divergent areas of study, although I had loved each one in its own right. From collecting objects on nature walks, through learning the history of medieval monasteries to meticulous drawings of primroses and insects, I was passionate about each subject. I didn't appreciate until adulthood their real significance until these disparate topics combined in the guise of natural history art to make absolute sense.

Growing up I developed a keen interest in art and making things. I remember as a young child finding an old bird's nest. As well as my fascination with its textures, I wondered at its extraordinary construction. I loved especially going on a nature walk and gathering small objects, plants and flowers and bringing them back to place on the table. I remember being encouraged to look at the textures and colours, and I always felt a connection with the objects. Even now, my pockets are always full of gathered treasures, feathers and oak galls.

Primroses in jam jars, bluebells and curled crooks of furry ferns still evoke a childlike pleasure – the names and folklore associated with the plants providing equally as much pleasure. For years I believed a childhood story that gooseberry hairs were used to make paintbrushes, and that glue is made from sticky buds of horse chestnut, finding touching these relentlessly shiny buds irresistible even as an adult. I still have to bend to pick tufts of pineapple weed to crush it and breathe in the sweetly pungent scent.

I have always been acutely aware of the seasons, their changes and symbolism: the silence of snow in winter; the verdant hope and possibility of spring; the long, hazy days of summer, with the scent of baked ground and swaying grasses in the verges; the feel of early autumn sun as we returned to school in September to start the new academic year. The experience is visceral.

Summers spent as a Girl Guide made a significant impression upon me. Learning to see and follow animal tracks and to spend time in the outdoors, using natural resources to make campfires and camp gadgets, will always be with me. Even now there will be wood that will be earmarked in case its shape is vital for the making of some piece of equipment. Camping and using the outdoors helped me not to take natural resources and our surroundings for granted, but to respect and treasure what they offer us.

The summer when the biology A-level field trip took place seemed endless, as did the field trip itself. In north Wales we had an idyllic time counting species growing in a square yard in a high meadow of Coed Hafod – which I recall translates as 'summer farm'. On another day we counted the species in a boggy meadow, and the cotton grass

Foxglove wild

and sundews were exciting finds. This file is one that I have kept from schooldays; and that, along with the biology practical file, is perhaps where the connection between the investigation, the 'find' and the recording is best seen. The thrill of looking to see if a primrose is pin-eyed or thrum-eyed is still a thrill. The three different presentations of the purple loosestrife still hold fascination.

This fascination has now transferred to the garden and landscape where I live. In fact, any lane or verge is of interest, and often it is a challenge to find a pull-off (easier in a Land Rover) in which to stop so that an orchid can be photographed to be identified later, and possibly drawn.

Although the preoccupation started in childhood, occupation as a botanical and natural history artist began in my mid-twenties – and has been a constant for over half my life, and certainly all of my adult life. Periodically exhibiting work, both on a group and – perhaps more pleasingly for oneself – solo basis; this is always an opportunity to contemplate and appraise, the exhibition experience providing punctuation in one's work, sometimes leading to new presentations or to completely new ideas.

I am very fortunate now to do something that I love; it is with me all the time, a private joy that goes on in my head even when not sitting painting. It's one at which I feel I can excel. For me the proof of this came in 2014 when I exhibited at the RHS and they decided that they, too, liked my work and awarded me a gold medal and the coveted 'best in show'. This is the same as a Chelsea gold medal but for botanical artwork. I remain delighted with this recognition. It provided an opportunity to reflect and take stock. Around this time I was also approached by two important collectors of botanical artwork, and their acquisition of my paintings was also a milestone for me; goals and aims I set myself privately some years ago were now being realised.

This gives some indication of my passion for and commitment to my artwork. I work really hard to create accurate, vivid paintings that show a plant or flower with integrity and vibrancy. Looking back, I can see that botanical and natural history painting has been a constant for me for much of my life, and has woven itself through various occupations until I knew what I was really meant to do: paint, and paint with a passion.

Having grown up on the southern edge of Hertfordshire, I now live in rural East Hertfordshire where we have a large conservation garden with meadow surrounding the 1640s thatched cottage that I describe in my preface, 'A Garden to Cherish'. I draw and paint in a studio in the grounds of my home. From here I can watch the wildlife and changing seasons. For me there is nothing better than having the excuse to wander the garden or green lanes and hedgerows in search of some gorgeous plant material, butterfly wing, feather or shell that demands to be painted.

The plants and trees within the garden and in the surrounding landscape provide inspiration and very often the subjects for

my work, as well as a huge collection of ephemeral matter (old hat, shoe and fragrance boxes make for excellent dry and dark storage).

Next to the larger studio is the smaller studio where I do most of my work. This is an old converted stable. Clad in rough-sawn timber and looking out across the fields to a huge landmark oak in the distance, it is a calm and tranquil space in which to work – heated by a basic wood burner and containing lovely old storage units where I can keep some of the material I use and that inspires me.

My other passions involve making textiles. The theme of texture, colour and form are also riven through everything I do or make. This is a passion bordering on obsession. I have done this for as long as I can remember, relishing natural materials and textures and getting lost in hand-dyed yarns and British-grown and woven woollen fabrics. My fibre collection competes with my paints and ephemera collection, and in my studio my old 1930s haberdashery cabinets house both painting and knitting and sewing materials. Plant materials and landscapes often provide inspiration for paintings and for garments, with colours influencing both artworks and also my next craft project. Textures provide ideas and inspiration, too, and paintings and garments come from the same places in my head and my heart. Both involve passion, attention to detail and a determination to succeed. A perfectionist by nature, I will doggedly persevere until the made object cannot be improved upon in my view.

In painting – as in sewing and knitting – I am largely colour and texture driven. By this I mean that the subject – whether a flower, insect, shell or feather – feels right and seems to speak to me until I take it into the studio to start work on it. I usually have an idea of how a finished piece will look. I also develop a feel for the layout as I want to recreate a place or a season on the paper simply with the natural objects I find around me.

I want my work to offer an interpretation of the garden and hedgerow landscape, through plants (and

Standing stone featuring Keats' words 'Four seasons fill the measure of the year' by lettercut artist Caitriona Cartwright

a few insects), captured for posterity on paper or vellum in watercolour. The plants and other subjects I paint are necessarily seasonal. Plants have lifecycles that are driven by the seasons. In the pursuit of reproduction they respond to conditions of light and temperature in order to grow, reproduce and set seed; so the subjects of my artwork necessarily tell the story of the year.

This book makes the connection between *place*: verge, hedgerow and garden; *time*: the season or month; and the *piece*: the act of selecting and articulating a plant by hand in paint on paper. Each plant and painting tells a story: my story, your story and the story of where we live, how we live in the land: season by season, it fills 'The Measure of the Year'.

A PERFECT IMPERFECTION

Botanical and natural history art are all about capturing the found object: first seek your object. The finding can take place anywhere, but the treasured found object is the one in your own home or garden. The found object will reflect its life, used, affected and then renounced by nature; and, like us, its imperfections are part of its story. The painting of the object in detail gives rise to a perfect imperfection.

The act starts within. It may be on a journey, perhaps on a lonely stretch of road, passing verges with hints of white (snowdrops in winter), chalky pale yellow (primroses), deeper shades of mustard (cowslips), sharp blues (bluebells), magenta (foxgloves), soft dilute blues (harebells), sunny yellows (toadflax)… these are the flowers of the nature table of childhood; the flower names carrying myths and legends of the natural kingdom.

From these dreamed beginnings, thoughts stir. Thoughts become images, evolving in direct opposition to the way in which dreams fade, becoming more elusive the more one tries to recall them.

And so a piece of artwork gestates within. It may gestate slowly, then be held in time, sometimes to fade away; or it may develop to become an idea, a concept and then a formed set of feelings that can be borne on to the paper or vellum.

The work is felt; the season imbibed and distilled until the found and captured object can be portrayed in all its perfect imperfection. Shapes, textures, colours and habits must be placed as the painting is made so that the object is depicted as it is; translucent or solid, rough or velvet, bowed or straight, meek or strong.

These reflect the processes that happen as the painting evolves. From glimpsed beginnings, into those half-remembered dreams, into a concept that can become a work. Made from the heart, this mix of hand and heart and head and eye.

The overarching theme in my work is the notion of the season, the time and the place. The 'imagery and symbolism' of the object. The subject of the painting is to take you to the hedgerow, verge or garden; remembering that subject and what it means to you. This is the symbolism. The imagery is the object; gossamer butterfly wings, a curled dead leaf or the velvet falls of iris.

Thus, this book and the images work through the seasons of the English countryside…

IT IS WINTER 2017. The lanes in rural Hertfordshire are covered in the whitest snow. Temperatures are below freezing,

Snowdrops, the February Fair Maids

and all nature is in abeyance. Snowdrops are captured beneath the snow. All narcissus are held, poised and paused.

A dormant time, a time of hibernation. But in such hibernation small stirrings begin. Germs of ideas grow, and new paintings start their journey. Small objects are glimpsed in hedgerow and in mind's eye: catkins, goat willow, gnarled and vibrant rose hips. Colours and textures are held on the tongue; an idea of the smallest sort begins. Like the formation of a word added to other words into a sentence, a conversation starts. Initially a soliloquy, as more ideas form a discourse starts. Shapes, texture and colour evolve.

The objects are taken into the studio and a long observation begins. Feeling, seeing and circumnavigating. Thoughts of colours emerge from the frost.

Cerulean blue mixed with pale lemon yellow – opaque and with some body colour, the flowering catkin can emerge. The closed catkin has cerulean with pale lemon and some rose doré – that most elusive and reticent of reds. The resultant mix is a blush that is neither green nor yellow, nor brown nor pink, but is all of these.

The goat willow stem is rich russet, gleaming cobalt teal blue sheen highlights and perylene violet with deep sea green. The flowers are the softest buff titanium, generous as the swan's down. The shadow of each filament is a different shade; phthalo blue, aureolin and vermilion mixed conservatively in various proportions to deliver soft and sharper greys.

The rose hips are rich. Like semi-precious stones they are the imperial topaz of the plant world. Rich and clear colours are required, overlaid and strong, the concept of the watercolour wash completely inadequate for these jewels of substance. Quinacridone yellow deep, carmine and perylene maroon red, gold brown are ideal for the depth of tone and form. Highlights may be cobalt violet or cobalt turquoise depending on the dominant colour of the hip.

As the travels within the paintbox begin, simultaneously form and spaces are contoured as a design takes shape in the mind's eye. Just like the half-remembered dream, small sketches may be needed or these fleeting ideas can disappear like early morning mist, hovering above the ground to vanish, snatched from the grasp.

Will the piece be on vellum or paper? Mostly the choice of the support is determined by the subjects themselves. They seem to choose. Vellum, being a natural and very organic material, seems

Gifts from the garden

to work with the most natural and wilder objects. Here the thought process becomes more visceral; hard to define and formed less of words and argument, and more of texture, form and colour.

The paint sits upon the surface of the vellum, defying washes and threatening to be removed by a too wet brush, just like the pollen on the hazel catkin can be washed away in a downpour.

After the observation has taken place – and there is no fixed time for this – the subject is placed and lightly sketched, often straight on to the surface with a fine HB. Lightly and softly. Initially I found such

mark-making difficult, such concentration transferring itself down my arm to the pencil, creating shapes too definite and ill at ease for my liking.

Sometimes I trace a shape in the air; a curve, an angle and then reflect this in pencil on paper. Sometimes allowing the shapes to develop and then to be traced off on to the precious vellum. Other times they go straight on, clear and decisive.

This is not fixed. It can be a question of finding a texture or colour that begs to be the way in. Either way, it is about making a good beginning. Well begun is half done. The greater the investment in the piece from

the start, the more decisive and diligent is the ongoing endeavour. Sometimes all the work is brought up a level, area by area; other times, a discrete area will be brought up to 85 per cent completion and then another area commenced. There is no fixed rule, and it is about whatever allows one to enter the work and to leave it between sittings in a 'good place'. The good place extending to the standard of the work as well as to the psychological place.

There is the fine balance between leaving the piece at the high point where it beckons you back, like an addict; and, if the piece is being difficult, to leaving well

Out soon

alone rather than persisting in a part of the work in a way that risks its quality and integrity… This is impossible to define, and marks out the skilled craftsman as opposed to the enthusiast. This aspect is about self-knowledge as much as about knowledge of the technical abilities. "Put down the brush and step away now…"

If a piece is being developed in splendid isolation then it can be painted to reach completion. Well, things are never really completed. As in nature we learn that the evolution goes on and on, so there is always an opportunity to do more. The trick is learning to identify the 'enough' that leaves the watercolour looking vibrant and fresh but not weak, the textures clear and defined without being overworked. This becomes more instinctive and sometimes fits with the season; allowing the potential of more growth in a spring subject is obvious. In winter there can be finality to the dead leaf and its textures and form.

The final stages of a piece of work, as in nature, are the fine details. Stamens, made up of filaments and anthers, need detail. This is being true to the craft of making the natural history painting. This detail comes with fine, round brushes and high-quality pigments. Last touches may be adding slight depth of colour to tone or texture like the pollen grains sitting on the anther. Most of us who practise this art form are driven by our observation; it is in this we revel, absorbed and preoccupied by the minutiae.

Hopefully, well-evolved imagery will be pleasing to the viewer and will evoke, symbolising season or place. Sometimes at this stage small additions may occur. Just as a scene in the hedgerow will be added to by an insect's presence, thus sometimes we find in the cabinet of curiosities the snail shell that complements the pheasant feather.

Rose petals   *Hydrangea in progress*

I give you my heart

WINTER

Four seasons fill the measure of the year;
There are four seasons in the mind of man:
He has his lusty Spring, when fancy clear
Takes in all beauty with an easy span:
He has his Summer, when luxuriously
Spring's honied cud of youthful thought he loves
To ruminate, and by such dreaming high
Is nearest unto heaven: quiet coves
His soul has in its Autumn, when his wings
He furleth close; contented so to look
On mists in idleness — to let fair things
Pass by unheeded as a threshold brook.
He has his Winter too of pale misfeature,
Or else he would forego his mortal nature.
John Keats – The Human Seasons (1818)

DECEMBER

There is a delicious sense of anticipation. The days are colder and shorter, the fire lit more frequently in the evenings. Colours are muted and often only shown in the short, intense bursts of slanting winter sun. Trees are brown in the gloom, and then all shades of ochre, green gold, burnt sienna, violet caput mortuum and umbers in the sun. The final golden pears fall heavily and provide nectar for the tortoiseshell butterflies. The holly has been laden with many berries, portentous of 'a hard winter' and also of the imminent season of goodwill and excitement. Wood pigeons and blackbirds rest on swaying boughs of holly and have usually all but stripped accessible branches of berries by Christmas. Any berried holly required for teaching, decorating or painting purposes must be obtained and kept in a bucket in a dark, cool stable until required.

The churchyard opposite boasts a rather lovely holly tree bearing variegated leaves and orange fruits, a sort of scarlet lake mixed with aureolin and glorious glowing orange. A small sprig of this has found its way into a painting on more than

one occasion. The flower beds look fairly bleak from the cosy kitchen, but on closer inspection there is colour and painting opportunity. Purple callicarpa nod on arching branches, and *Viburnum davidii* boasts metallic indanthrene berries. There is a lovely paint colour called 'lunar blue' which looks for all the world as if made of these berries. The viburnum leaves are evergreen and deeply ridged. Privet fruits are glossy and black, unnoticed from afar, but obvious close up; and ivy berries are a matte blue green turning through indigo to deep black as they provide an unlikely avian feast.

The last roses bring much needed colour, often diminutive but still there, and a happy and welcome addition to a seasonal painting, perhaps alongside vintage baubles or ivy. The garden delivers a wealth of cones in December. These pleasing shapes are a joy to draw and paint; following spirals and reminding us of life in their facsimile of the double helix of DNA, these hold the life force of new trees and possibilities.

The bare trees provide form and structure and give rise to ideas for prints to be made and rolled through the heavy etching press next year.

After the festivities there is the fallow period between Christmas and New Year when next year's Christmas card can be planned or started, when dreams of new paintings can begin; and so the year ends and a new year starts with all its possibilities and opportunities as surely as leaves will unfurl and flowers bloom with reassuring regularity and reliance: "Four seasons fill the measure of the year".

BELOW, FROM FAR LEFT Winter treasures and mistletoe; Winter treasures and holly; Orange Holly study sheet

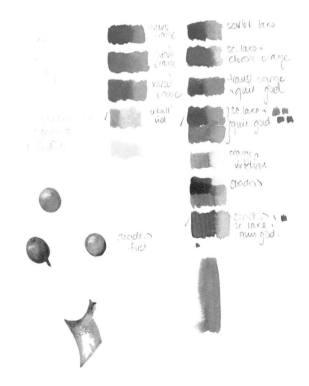

Pashley Manor (rose) and the mistletoe

JANUARY

The first task in January is to take forward the idea for this year's Christmas card, which germinated as the old year drew to a close. This is a delightful time to think about painting a card when there are none of the usual pressures associated with the season, for by now it is done with. The garden is held in abeyance with small treasures gleaming in the hedgerow or in the borders. From a distance the garden is dormant, mostly greens, green browns and greys. On closer inspection, the pearl-cream greens of the Christmas Rose sit close to the ground so that cold winds cannot bend them over and the fickle rains of that laconic time between Christmas and New Year cannot combine with the wind to push their faces into the muddy border.

A few holly berries still shine forth, a glorious red neither pink nor orange but that perfect pillar-box glossy bright red. The smaller branches luckily cannot support the weighty grey-green pigeons that have gorged themselves on most of these fruits. In fact, if holly required for Christmas decorations within the cottage is not gathered in by late November then it is too late; just these few remaining berries begging to be captured by the paintbrush.

These jewels of mid-winter sit well with small wishbones of mistletoe, which dry to a bronze green reminiscent of silk taffeta of a long forgotten bridesmaid's dress described as 'chartreuse'. The berries of the mistletoe are a lovely pearl-grey cream green.

Mosses and lichens adorn the lawn as victims of high winds blown down from lofty boughs. Several large trees have succumbed to the weather, and bows have become weighed down by the heft of wet snow; momentary in nature, and in just seconds, the bow cracks away and falls. The lichens are gathered up into a basket; and, after drying, display well in glass jars in the studio, their soft grey green found in few other natural objects.

Catkins dance and shiver in chill January winds, tight peachy green, opening to softer yellow greens covered in powdery pollen. Daisies sporadically decorate the lawn amongst bright-green mosses that give evidence of the cold and wet winter months. Snow falls fast and quiet overnight, cloaking the garden, field and hedgerows. Fieldfares and redwings take on brighter colours against the sparkling white snow as they forage for food in the hedges and through the fallen leaves. Wrens and robins and all finches and tits clamour for space on the feeders, providing welcome distraction and colour in the oft-dull January days.

Rabbits and weasels, looking coarse and regal, respectively, make use of the garden as a playground and marketplace; at

Cone of the eastern white pine

Cone II

night a badger gains entry, pushing his (or her) way through pig and chicken wire and ineffectual piles of leaves left stacked in vain against the fence.

Favourite painting subjects at this time are dried treasures – contained in glass cases, specimen jars, display cabinets and many shoe boxes – as well as long-dead insects, shells, feathers, broken and discarded bird eggs.

Shiny beetles, small baubles and dried rosebuds are to the natural history painter as precious stones are to the jeweller – a source of wonder and inspiration; pleasure gained just from the looking, and optimism for spring and summer obtained.

FROM TOP The bauble; The bauble II

FEBRUARY

In February, just when you think that the hellebores have died and that the snowdrops have vanished beneath their blanket of annual leaf mould, small clumps of bright-green leaves appear, spiking up through the blanket of sepia-toned leaves. Disconcertingly, they just look green, and on closer inspection there is really no sign of flowers; perhaps just the odd oval bud, enough to give slight pleasure, but not enough for proper optimism. Suddenly, usually in mid-February, small white flowers gleam against their inky backcloth. As if by magic, their numbers swell and entire clumps of flowers are there, each clump numbering up to thirty flowers.

Near them, in the part of the garden we call 'The Ride', pale yellow-green hellebores arch up, keeping their freckled faces modestly bowed. Occasional large and slow bumblebees ponderously browse these nectar-laden blooms, giving rise to optimism and joy. In other parts of the garden, deep and dark hellebores reflect blacks, reds and ruddy browns and muddy dark pinks. Always there is green in the mix and a bronzy quality that gives a hint as to the photosynthesising function of these misnamed 'petals'.

Birds in their fine winter coats grace the feeders: long-tailed tits, blue tits, chaffinches, robins and, most dapper, the great spotted

The final medlars

woodpecker. The pheasants strut beneath the feeders hoping for dropped fragments of nut and seed.

In the flower beds the daphne is pinkly fragrant, joined by wintersweet and the crepe papery petals of witch hazels. The last of the rose hips are shades of orange browns and gold ochres, occasionally a blue black as if made of unpolished jet; a joyful surprise.

Fallen leaves still grace the paddock; and the odd oak leaf clings, smooth and

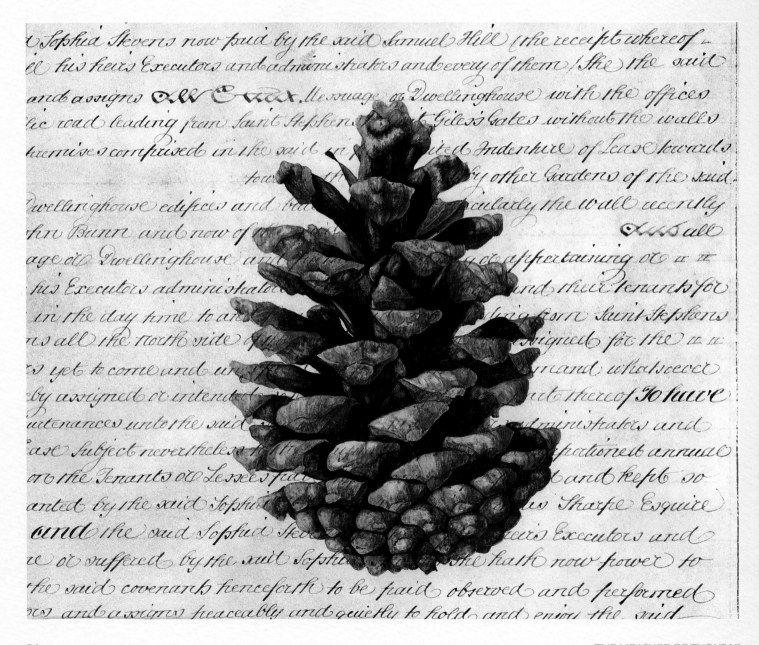

FROM LEFT Palimpsest fir cone;
Christmas rose, holly and mistletoe

Rosa glauca hips

brown rustling gently in the breeze. It is a perfect time of year to conceive paintings of found objects of seasons past; rooting through boxes of treasure is akin to going through grandma's button box.

More snow seems to cloak the daffodil spikes and, as if insulating them, encourages their growth so that when the snow melts they appear to have pushed further into the light. One or two have opened and the icy weather makes them translucent, bows their faces to the ground, and they only climb skywards once more after the thaw and a little warming sun.

The first bullfinches appear, and we see the very first one of the year perched in the lee of the wind on our thatch, just outside a window. A decadent and joyous rosy presence, he tones well with the patterned silk curtain fabric. The odd bumblebee is spotted hovering impossibly slowly around the nectar-laden hellebores, but this year the brimstone butterfly is as yet unseen.

The goat willow flowers prolifically, transitioning from silver grey to abundant soft yellow as its stamens push out with their pollen-laden anthers.

Natural truth – Ivy leaves and bumblebee

ABOVE Snowdrops II; RIGHT Hellebore, feather and snail

February jewels

FACING PAGE My heart's beside the sea; ABOVE LEFT Winter treasures and magnolia; ABOVE RIGHT The February heart

SPRING

Spring finds

MARCH

As if in contagion, the dafffodils open; a few each night, and soon they number too many to be counted – gleaming aureolin, that most reliable, consistent and pure of yellows. Aconites open their faces to the watery sun and are a far more acidic yellow, altogether more acerbic and shiny. Their green ruffs are a harsher green; and perhaps these stark, rudimentary colours are necessary in these diminutive flowers as they make them more noticeable. For all their brash colours they are a welcome addition and gladden the heart as each year they spread themselves further.

The *Leucojum*, or 'snowflakes', grace the garden, much taller than the snowdrops; this is fitting as they are perhaps still in transit as if the 'flake' is still falling from the sky.

Celandines start to compensate for the loss of the winter aconites, and themselves are a slightly warmer acid yellow – just a hint of warmth in them. Late snow for two days makes the long-tailed tits incongruous as they clutch long pieces of grass thatch in their mouths as they begin nest-building preparations.

Thrushes are also starting the nesting process. Leaf buds on all the trees begin to show colour, giving truth to the promise of spring, although they remain tiny. The exception to this is the *Magnolia soulangeana*. This mature tree has a glorious structure, and this is mossy and lichenous against a dark *lonicera* hedge, the pale ochre green suede buds looking for all the world like a thousand small lights waiting to be lit. The anticipation of

Faithfulness eases my heart

Modesty befits her sweet beauty

Muscari macrocarpum

Daffodil trio

the large cream, peach pink flowers is countered by disquiet about the April and May frost that can turn the entire tree completely brown, seemingly in a moment. An upsetting consequence of our desire to have the world's trees in our view and grasp; our control of the garden is made a mockery by our powerlessness over the weather.

Violets give scent and colour in the place where garden and hedgerow merge. Crouching in the long grass they look tiny, but have surprisingly long stems when plucked. Their fragrance is momentary, apparently containing a pheromone that once smelt means it can no longer be sensed, until the next time.

Grape hyacinths contrast well with the violets, their bluer violets and baby blues with rich sap greens call for the use of cobalts and ultramarines when painting them. A small posy of these with a few violets and small hellebore buds is very welcome on the kitchen table in the oft-dull days of March.

At last the equinox nears and clocks go forward, reminding us that things are changing even if the winter feels long, cold and fairly dull; light levels and day lengths will both increase, as inevitable as ever.

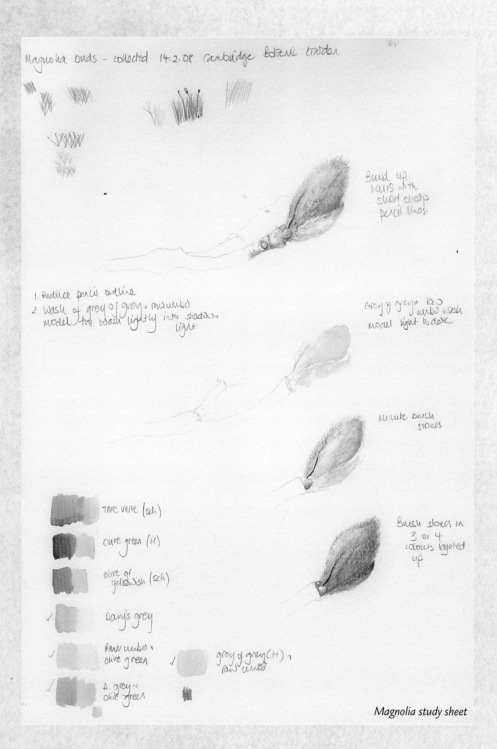

Magnolia study sheet

APRIL

Just when one believes that it is only in the photographs and memories of past years that the garden will grow, a few warm days, or even just hours, are sufficient for growth. Warmed earth and gentle rain add their elements, and alchemy occurs. From creamy hints the magnolia swells and opens; impossibly large, waxy petals untwist from firm suede buds lined in the softest, sheeny glove leather.

As the bright yellows of the first daffodils fade, softer and kinder yellows emerge prior to the cream whites and tangerine centres of pheasant eye. The odd clump of jonquils opens, begging to be cut and placed in a jug to add a sweet scent to the kitchen.

The huge pear tree bears thousands of pale jade colour buds. All the better for the bullfinch; there are plenty to go round, and a few stolen buds make for fewer pears to rake up in autumn but leave enough for the feeding butterflies to feast upon prior to hibernation. The silver blossom will open as if late spring snow has fallen upon just this tree. She will shimmer and bear her coat as she has done for about four hundred years, according to our tree man, a fact we readily believe.

Bluebells start to grace the paddock and wilder parts of the garden, with a fair number of escapees in the beds. Despite our best efforts, the more upright and pale Spanish bluebells threaten our dominion; however, after months of dull browns and varied greens, that can only be determined when the sun does shine – all colour is welcome here. The English

Daffodil and bud

Magnolia buds

bluebell with her ultraviolet and cobalt mixed flowers nods with all her blooms on one side of her stalks, heads bent over as if in supplication. Leaves that have stood upright are recumbent as if in awe of their flower-bearing counterparts.

This month is when we first hear the cuckoo. Not every year but most years. Thrilled to hear her call, we ignore how this signals marauding behaviour, when she will turf out unceremoniously the eggs of the host bird who will raise these 'foundling children' unknowing that they are not her own. One year we watched a blackbird feeding a recalcitrant pair of cuckoo chicks, first believing this to be some special dance between the blackbird and much larger thrushes, until we realised the 'gigantic' other birds showed not mottling but the chest barring of the cuckoo.

A few clumps of cowslips open here and

Shades of Magnolia –
soulangeana

Shades of Magnolia –
Liliiflora nigra

there, their scent filling the air around them on warmer days. The banks of ditches nearby are swathed in these pretty flowers, having only recently looked barren with just the odd velvety, basal rosette for confirmation that the cowslips ever grow there.

The holly is in flower in late April into early May, and the Holly Blue butterfly will lay her first clutch of eggs on this spiky host. Bluebells grow beneath the holly trees in our garden; and last year's fallen bronzy leaves sit amidst the bluebells, giving rise to an idea for a painting. The tracery of the veining in the leaves is as if cast in bronze, and a play on words delivers a composition: bluebell, holly and the Holly Blue.

Violets seem to have died back and then their small, hopeful faces light up shady nooks beneath heavy greenery. What to paint? Certainly a different palette is called for: sharp acid yellows give way to softer, warmer yellows, a little hint of scarlet within them, as if the sun has warmed the yellows. Blues and cool violets start to

Narcissi and the pheasant feather (on backing sheet)

show, and greens change from glaucous blue greens of earlier spring to the grassier greens of bluebells. First tree foliage is so-called 'spring green', a colour that is hard to believe at other times of the year. Transparent yellows and cobalts mix to a sharp, clear green, slightly offset by a dab of scarlet lake to render the greens limey and vibrant, seemingly glowing as if having taken on a hint of the radiating sun.

Bluebells, holly and the Holly Blue

MAY

Fritillaria meleagris, or snake's head fritillaries, are open and abundant. Sadly, each flower seems made imperfect by the curious pheasant. The bestial name of these flowers belies their beauty, and their heads nod in the gentle May breeze amidst the pheasant eye narcissus, contributing to the menagerie of the old damp pond beneath an old, old walnut, an ash and varied conifers.

Birds are noisy companions in the garden, from dawn until dusk. Nest-building goes on in earnest; the lawn is scarified for its abundant moss, each foray leaving an untidy mound of moss where some has been plucked. The green woodpeckers add to this by seeking leather jackets and ants within the grass, favouring the early-morning stillness for most of their gathering.

Foxglove leaves in large velvety mounds seem to swell daily and the flower spikes push up; some years more white, and

Snake's head fritillary

Spring posy I; Spring posy II

Fritillaries and bee

some years more purple. A small foxglove bought some years ago from Gilbert White's garden at Selborne remains in the memory more than it does in the garden. She was a foxy and beguiling shade of sherbet lemon: lemon yellow titanate and dilute carmine and magenta. Her bee line spots, as if painted, are a deep perylene violet. In clear light the flowers or 'gloves' gleam and shimmer with a crystalline effect that seems especially present in the flowers of late spring.

Irises are a favourite painting subject, and many happy hours have been spent pouring over the selections in nurseries and at specialist growers. I have found that south-facing beds, backed by a protective *lonicera* hedge, are a suitable location for my iris collection. It is an unnerving joy to watch as the fans of sword-like leaves push up from the rhizomes, adding an incredible length on warmer days.

With bated breath one waits to see if there is any swelling at the base of the sword fan. If there is, then it is a flower spike. Often one feels sadness as the

Foxglove after Arthur Harry Church

Digitalis purpurea 'Alba'

Digitalis purpurea 'Sutton's Apricot'

fan seems devoid of growth and then suddenly a swelling starts and a flower spike emerges. Oh, one thinks, perhaps it will not be very great; but, then, as if propelled by a magic force, it gains speed and girth and colour and a tall, flowering spike is there, waist high – sometimes very nearly head high. These flowers are shortlived, and the very first one I ever painted, 'Action Front', took nearly four years, if one included the very first year of purchasing and drawing... Since then, irises have become a firm favourite, their flower shapes and structures providing a rich harvest of painting subjects.

They usually require a rich palette, and all the boxes of paints are open, from emerald and viridian greens to deep purples to peach to perylenes and quinacridones of every hue. Huge wads of paint must be squeezed out into the palette; no dainty brush tips of colour here. Whole petals wetted and swathes of colour applied, large brush, with gusto. The reserve of winter and spring has left, and colour confidence abounds. It is wise, however, to have a test paper on the go, so as not to get carried away on the best paper with a painstakingly drawn

composition, with a wet and loaded brush, as one happily binges on the colours of the iris.

Tulips also provide colour and pleasing shapes and textures. The catalogues and websites in autumn provide a colourful bounty and tempt us with groaning baskets of bulbs. It is known for there to be an excess of bulb-buying enthusiasm over bulb-planting capacity, and sometimes labelling goes awry. Although a delight, these flowers, which tend to fade to blues and violets as they decay, cannot, in my view, beat the lovely iris.

Nesting birds abound, and every morning I watch, soon after rising, a female blackbird approach a huge box ball with grassy thatch and moss in her mouth. She flies in about four yards from the box. She sits and looks from left to right, and if she is happy that she is unobserved she will fly to the top of the box ball and enter – with some difficulty, for her width, mouth full of nest makings, extends to some six inches. I vow to snoop on her efforts while she is out collecting again, but usually forget.

The tits are in every nest box, and a hole in the laburnum tree provides a lovely space for a nest. When the sun sinks towards the west it lights up the

BELOW Digitalis I; RIGHT Iris 'Red Orchid'

nest, and when parents nip away for food a quick view shows several gaping beaks. Further round this tree is a thrush's nest. I wonder how many families this tree supports. Its form always makes me think of Enid Blyton's *The Magic Faraway Tree*.

Woodpeckers whiz round and round. A large green woodpecker spends up to thirty minutes scarifying the lawn – it is hard to feel cross about the mess, and he then has a good bath in the pond, somehow slipping off the small escape stone to become fully immersed. Much splashing and shaking and he is out again – looking around to see if his undignified mishap was witnessed. Stray woodpecker feathers are a favourite and special find in the garden, requiring to be added to the collection of ephemera and then to be painted. Surprisingly time-consuming to paint and draw, their yellow greens, dark-grey browns and cream spots make a smart combination.

Apple blossom bursts from pale buds (best painted with nickel titanate yellow and cerulean blue mixed), and its fresh washing-powder scent is pure pleasure. The bullfinch is once again welcome and bright, the coral breast clashing pleasantly with the pink of the apple blossom.

Perhaps the favourite plant this month

is the modest but effusive cow parsley. Each year I am dismayed that this lovely structural plant has disappeared from the wild, longer-grassed areas, and then suddenly there she is, tight bright-green buds curled and then opening frothy white umbels. These are a delightful subject for printmaking, especially etching, and then in winter the seedheads of the wild carrot, the cow parsley and the hogweed provide good painting material.

The swifts and swallows are here, swooping in their familiar flight; seemingly tireless after their epic journey.

These two paintings were created at the same time as the country was divided about the referendum vote for leaving or staying in the EU. Some of the flowers leant towards one another and others leant apart: it felt as though they provided a metaphor for the heartfelt views and feelings that leavers or remainers held; hence 'standing together' (overleaf) and 'standing apart' (pages 60-61).

Standing together – deep black

Standing apart – breathing fire

The butterscotch iris

Iris 'Pink Pele'

FACING PAGE Iris 'Sable' I
RIGHT The deep purple iris

Iris 'Red Rufus'

THE MEASURE OF THE YEAR

Iris 'Quechee'

Iris 'Benton Caramel'

Umbels II

SUMMER

JUNE

Suddenly the year is bolting. It was winter, then spring, then… June. It is summer. Not all the days are summery, and sometimes there is a chill wind and a dull sky; but there are light, bright mornings and bird song fills the air from dawn 'til dusk. The roses, from having glossy leaves and lots of growth, suddenly have swelling buds. Lots of them. There is an impatience within to see those buds open and for the sun to warm them and release the peppery, lemony scent. There is nothing lovelier than burying your nose within a warm, open rose and breathing in her summer scent.

This brings memories of childhood when there seemed nothing wrong with 'making' perfume from the roses. Pulling off petals, only perfect ones you understand, and then placing them into a jam jar – possibly the one that had until recently contained the caterpillar and its food or a chrysalis – with water, likely from the water butt, so therefore full of mosquito larvae and already carrying a sweet smell of decay. Sadly, the rose

The song of the rose

The June heart

Rose, thrush's egg and feather

petals soon turned brown and the smell of the 'perfume' was most unpleasant, nearly matched by the reprimand for pulling off the rose petals.

The hedgerows boast the country cousin of the garden roses, the dog rose in her various forms. This time of year makes me think fondly of the cover of Keble Martin's wild flower book and how simple yet comprehensive are his drawings and the information contained therein. Still and always a joy to take on any walk.

Near the stables the honeysuckle scents the night air. A straggly and untidy wild thing, curled all round a holly oak near the cattle trough, she is like a schoolgirl with a growth spurt – suddenly all long legs and reaching up to the sky. The flowers are yellow and white, sadly not blushed with rose doré.

The foxgloves are fully out – in the hedgerow and in the garden, a most welcome wild flower. In different years they have different patterns, sometimes

tall and robust, other years smaller and with several spikes from one basal rosette. Perhaps like the bluebells, they are best glimpsed at dusk when their white spires appear to hover above the ground like long candle beacons.

In amongst the grass the speedwell grows, alongside daisies, clover and self heal. Docks and grasses start to flower; the colours in these are surprising, the grass pollens often grey violet or magenta, and the dock or sorrel bright carmine. Dead nettle is a creamy white, and in the paddock works well with the bluebells and the fairy ring of toadstools near the oak tree.

From dusk the owls hoot, 'towhit, towhoo', the calls of a pair, and they can be heard clearly in the garden. Sadly, their favourite maple was victim to winter gales so they have to use the old pear and conifers. For some months the bathroom windowsill was a night-time roost for an owl, leaving interesting pellets to be examined in the morning.

From the collection 1

Rosa reconciliation from behind

JULY

The rose arbour continues to bloom, its earlier tidy chicness replaced with a bucolic feel of midsummer. Hotter and lazier days with a gentler buzz of insects audible on the air. Butterflies swoop and glide amongst the sweet blooms of privet, drunkenly sipping nectar and warming themselves in the sun. The air smells of hot, dry earth, if not for the whole month at least for some of the time.

We are lucky with an abundance of butterflies: commas, tortoiseshells, fritillaries, painted ladies, red admirals, skippers and gatekeepers. Peacocks have bred in the paddock on the swathes of hairy stinging nettles, and are perhaps our most frequent visitors. Indeed, not visitors; rather, this is their home.

The grasses in the paddock flower, their dusty mauve heads nodding gently in a summer breeze, looking generous and rich and a far cry from the short and damp tussocky grasses from late autumn until spring.

Treecreepers and nuthatches can be seen, as if the tree bark is alive and moving. They use the dappled shade to good effect, but you can get your eye in and see them quite clearly

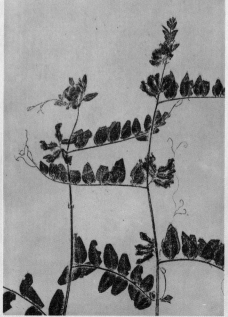

Rosa 'Munstead Wood'

seeking out small insect morsels.

The vetch twists and turns, its tendrils clasping on itself, until, top heavy, it tumbles to begin its climb anew, forming a delightful mass of sinuous tendrils and curves which prove good shapes to use in etchings that have the very feel of field boundaries.

Within the garden beds the hydrangeas start to bloom. Mostly shades of pink, white and green, our soil not supporting the more unusual blues and turquoises, they still provide a dramatic display. They grow in front of a huge ball of a yew tree, and in the front of the bed is a lovely oak settle, its back shaped in gothic arches that echo the windows of the house.

Other beds host achillea, thalictrum and shrubs, providing interesting shades of green, dark reds and coppers.

Rosa 'Mutabilis'

Artichoke

AUGUST

The greens in both garden and hedgerow begin to change this month. Hints of red in the greens start them on their journey towards autumn, and the greens turn towards khaki and olive. The leaves take on a tired look, as they are two-thirds of the way through their life.

In the verges the hogweeds turn from fresh green with cream flowerheads to shades of dirty lime, and as the giant heads set seed they become every shade of umber, ochre, sepia with hints of violet and silver blue. Looking ochre-grey brown from a distance, these majestic heads have many colours in their slightly twisted seeds. They sit at the end of each umbrella spoke and seem metallic. In fact, the addition of mineral pigments into paint mixes gives just the right texture and feel when painting them.

The grasses sway lazily in the heat that can come in August days, and take me back to school holidays where the endless

The rose and the woodpecker

days could be spent drifting around the local wild areas, stick in hand – for some reason pulling the stick along the hollow corrugated stems of hogweed and cow parsley – and on occasion bashing them to see and hear their seeds scatter far and wide.

Local growers sell dahlias by the bucket load on the side of the lane. These flowers remind me of my grandfather who used to grow them. I never liked their huge heads, or their colours, but now their association with childhood and the colours, reminiscent of 1960s floral fabrics have a

charm that I cannot resist. A large bunch will set you back just £5 for Help for Heroes – I think how much these would cost in a florist, and happily pay four times that much to such a good cause.

Some of the local fields are swathed in poppies, shimmering in the sunlight, their

FACING PAGE, FROM LEFT
Alchemilla moon; Dancing girl
from Shotley Peninsula
THIS PAGE *Rosa 'Just Joey'*

papery petals sheeny and catching the sun. Other fields boast the cool blues of flax, and where the poppies crowd into the flax field (and there are ripe cornfields adjacent) the patchwork fields look unbelievable and as though painted by an over-enthusiastic colourist.

Our paddock manages to carry buttercups well into August, and along the paddock edges small swathes of thistle (all the better for the goldfinches) and the rosebay willowherb remind us that spring is far behind us and that autumn is imminent. Another kind of

yellow is present in the paddock, much loathed by every horse owner: the ragwort. Food plant of the cinnabar moth caterpillar, a few of these are worth keeping to support this black and red moth as well as to use as a dye plant.

The paddock is host to many

Pashley Manor and the feather

The deep red Guinee

butterflies; orange tips skip around the waist-high grasses. Hedge woundwort, a deadnettle relative, graces the shady areas beneath our huge lime trees and horse chestnut. They are well worth closer inspection as their flowers carry very detailed markings and for me are like a poor man's wild orchid. Teasels start to change from minty green with lilac flowers to a drier green brown, and they remind one that in years gone by they were used by spinners to 'tease' fleece or 'tops' into fibres which could be spun into yarn.

The roadside trees of sorbus or rowan start to bear fruit, and one's mind can turn, once again, to days of painting autumn subjects and evenings of knitting. Ideas of colours and textures influenced by the plants around.

On the chalky verges on the very edge of the Chilterns – or the East Anglian heights, as they are

optimistically called – toadflax and harebells flower alongside clover, wild yarrow or achillea of many shades, as if the wild flowers are having a last hurrah before the nights creep in and chills fill the evening air. Other verges, noted as ancient hill forts with 360 degree views, support broomrapes, a dramatic parasitic plant with no green parts. They look exotic with

colours of copper, orange and yellow ochre, like the invading soldiers in whose footsteps they tread.

In the paddock the first acorns are green and fresh, and if not harvested for painting purposes will succumb to the greedy squirrels. A few oak galls give cause for excitement, and plans of making inks from them to use in artwork provide yet

another aim that may not be realised as I have an excess of ideas over time.

In the hedgerows hips start to redden, with robin's pin cushions giving yet more cause for excitement. Mulberries and the first apples are ready in the garden as well as a few damsons – usually quite tart – but in warm sun they will have some sweetness and are a happy sign of the

The Oak gall

Roses in Willow pattern jug

autumn wild fruit harvest yet to come. As wild birds start the moult, feathers are frequent and welcome finds.

At the end of August we usually travel to the Great Dorset Steam Fair, which has been held for the last 50 or so years on a sweeping plain in the middle of the county. The ground has been farmed and the crops harvested. The fields are dusty with dry earth; and the sharp, stick-like stems of the cut corn scratch the ankles. Almost everyone can remember those intoxicating days at summer's end when walks across ploughed fields meant scratched ankles and boots covered in the dust of still dry earth. The drive home from Dorset is a happy time; sun-reddened cheeks tingle as one travels along the A30, eastwards away from the setting sun. The land is cast in glorious late summer sun at evening's end, symbolic of the passing of summer; and thoughts turn to paintings for the new season, autumn.

FACING PAGE *Around the meadow II; BELOW Around the meadow III*

Dahlia juliet from behind

Dahlia tamburo from behind

Rose in summer and autumn

Reconciliation in bud

GLS
MMX

SEPTEMBER

September starts as summer and ends as autumn, to my mind. Village shows of garden harvests abound, and such shows can still be visited in summer attire. The first taught workshops are usually planned for this month, and there is a sense of anticipation – a new-term sort of feel.

Planning starts in earnest for these workshops, with painting and handout preparation, as well as an amount of 'deadheading' of old painting material and demonstration sheets from last year, kept 'just in case'.

One particular handout (*Drawing and Painting Hedgerow Fruits*) is full of possibility, and planning for such workshops at the start of the term brings with it the pleasant obligation to wander lanes and tracks as well as to forage within the wilder parts of the garden for subject matter.

Ideas and compositions abound as if recalling a whole series of new paintings. These are worth noting as, often, thinking I will remember an idea, it fades like a dream upon waking. Whisp-like series of good ideas effervesce and then, like autumn mist wicked away by the early sun, they are gone. Sometimes such ideas re-emerge, and I usually think that the good idea will grow within one's head and heart, and if worthy of further exploration will develop into a painting or, more usually, a series of paintings.

I see September as a month of rebirth rather than as a month of decay. Perhaps for me the fruits are symbolic

DRAWING AND PAINTING HEDGEROW FRUITS

You can consider sketchbook-type work where you capture various details of the plant, such as sketches, enlargements and some painted parts.

Painting

Mix colours carefully. Often, wild fruits and flowers have small parts, but these may need clear colours. Alternatively, some may need larger washes of clear colour, such as quince.

If you do not wish to paint a whole plant, you can paint some parts, perhaps fading out and concluding stem and basal leaves in pencil.

TIP

Make sure you have spare fruits so that you can cut them open and see the colours inside. Often a plum will have a yellowy-green flesh, and this influences your choice of colours you might use for the skin. Sometimes a colour is hard to capture convincingly (eg, hawberry colour). The flesh of these small fruits is orangey yellow, and if you paint an underwash of that colour beneath the red they can look more convincing.

Hedgerow subjects

Here are some of the fruits and nuts that can be found at this time of year:

crab apple, damson, holly, walnut, rosehips, greengage, ivy, cobnut, wild apple, quince, mistletoe, mulberry, wild pear, bullace, haw, honeysuckle, blackberry, cornus, medlar, guelder rose, old man's beard, sloe, acorn, mountain ash.

Some useful colours for fruits:

COLOUR	POSSIBLE USES
W&N Quinacridone gold	Autumn leaves
W&N transparent yellow	Pears Apples Quince Crab apples – especially butterball and golden hornet
W&N green gold	Autumn leaves (to give a goldy/greeny glow over autumn leaves)
Schmincke translucent orange	Rose hips, autumn leaves
W&N scarlet lake	Rose hips, autumn leaves
Indigo	Sloes
Sepia	Autumn leaves Twigs and bark As a shadow mixed with a yellow for yellowy fruit, e.g. quince
W&N Perylene violet	In blackberries and mixed with a dark green to make a 'botanical black'
W&N Perylene green	Can be mixed with a yellow to give rich dark greens e.g. holly or ivy. Can be mixed with P. Violet to make a rich 'botanical black'
W&N Perylene maroon	Deep rich dark blood red, useful and richer alternative to alizarin crimson. Autumn leaves
Cerulean blue	Bloom on sloes, damsons, bullace and plums

of regeneration and the promise of new life. Traveller's joy and old man's beard abound along the lanes' edges. Ferns start to change from greens to russets, and arum fruits from bright acid greens to rich, bright, glowing orange. The guelder rose, the aptly named *Viburnum opulus*, is indeed opulent, its translucent warm red heads of fruits often pulling the stem down towards the earth. *Iris foetidissima* sheds her fruits via twisting and turning the fruit casing, which is made from a rich brown suede material. Buckthorn,

yew, dogwoods, horse chestnut and the romantically named 'wayfaring' tree all require different elements from the paint palette. Roses are still plentiful, and bringing their sweetly scented heads inside to paint is a pleasure always.

Later in the month the hydrangeas start to change. A favourite of mine, I painted a series of them through autumn and winter to exhibit with the Royal Horticultural Society. It was a real pleasure and joy to see them turn through greens, deep reds, blues and

dark turquoises. I still have some of the very heads I used for the paintings, some cut and gathered by arrangement from Caerhays in Cornwall late one September and placed in the boot of the Land Rover, with two very inquisitive cocker spaniels not understanding why quite so many heads were required.

I had enquired of the nursery about a few different types. I had been assured that they were in stock, and so had arranged to visit to collect my purchases. When I arrived the plants were indeed

Sign of the times – September

Orange rose II

Rosebud on Rory McEwen vellum II

Orange rose I

Rosebud on Rory McEwen vellum I

Rosa 'Grace'

THE MEASURE OF THE YEAR

in stock. However, they were not the colours I had been expecting. Apparently, a new recruit to the garden had planted them into normal compost and not into the acid-rich compost they favour. The plants I had chosen had grown dark, rich carmine and not the blue that I was seeking. I had planned my collection of paintings so that the work reflected varied colours as well as different characteristics within the hydrangea group. I was so disappointed. In the event this misfortune changed to good fortune as the staff came with me to the estate and, secateurs in hand, we set about dead-heading the very flower heads I needed. My painting of 'enziandom' remains one of my favourites – not least because of how the heads were snipped from the huge pyramidal bushes, popped unceremoniously into the back of the car and gently dried on the 350-mile journey home.

My write-up of *Hydrangea altona* found its way into the Edinburgh Botanic Garden publication 'The Botanics', and from there the Hunt Institute in

LEFT Hydrangea macrophylla 'Altona'
FACING PAGE, LEFT Hydrangea
macrophylla 'King George'
FACING PAGE, RIGHT Hydrangea
macrophylla 'Renate Steiniger'

Pittsburgh, USA, picked up the story. They contacted me asking to acquire the painting. So, in the event, what a happy accident that mis-planting in Cornwall was. I now have work within the International Collection of Botanical Documentation, known by all botanical artists just as 'The Hunt', and a place in whose collection we all aspire to be.

In September our garden offers few flowers, but a favourite is the autumn crocus. Ours has a chequerboard pattern on her petals, opening in the autumn sunshine and closing at the end of each day. She lasts longer than you would think possible for such a delicately petalled flower. We have not planted her and she springs up, looking like nothing much in the middle of lawn. Initially, one looks from the window wondering if some sweet wrapper has blown into the garden from afar. One's curiosity piqued, a venture into the garden fills the heart with joy as I realise it is the little colchicum.

Hydrangea macrophylla 'Masja'

Hydrangea macrophylla 'Pimpernel'

Hydrangea macrophylla 'Ayesha'

Hydrangea macrophylla 'General de Vicomtesse de Vibraye'

Hydrangea macrophylla 'Blaumeise'

Hydrangea macrophylla 'Mme Emile Mouillère'

Hydrangea macrophylla 'Alpengluhen'

Hydrangea macrophylla 'Nikko Blue'

I love you rose

OCTOBER

October means clocks changing and giving up the thought that there will be warmth other than for a fleeting hour in the middle of the day. The days draw noticeably shorter, and the dew falls heavy on the still-long grass. The scents of autumn start this month. Dew combined with lush grass and falling leaves give off an earthy odour, thoughts turning to decay as well as to the rebirth that the leaf mould will support.

Woody nightshade berries, jewel-red ovals and menacing shine brightly, hanging like gemstones on a necklace. A similar colour but sticky and translucent are the honeysuckle fruits, borne in clusters and more akin to a brooch in their presentation.

The first sloes are small and a dullish blue black. Too early for picking for sloe gin, they need the first frosts or a quick nip in the freezer to make them suitable for making this winter tipple. The leaves of the sloe are oval, and in October they turn from green to greeny yellow and then to a warmish naples yellow, which sit well with the blue fruits. As autumn winds move the branches, the leaves rub off the bloom on the fruits and they become scuffed and show the gleaming black

With Annette in my mind; full circle

that sits beneath the bloom. Notoriously difficult to paint, the clues for colours are all within.

Cut this fruit and the most delicious chartreuse colour is within the flesh. This, combined with ultramarine or indanthrene, gives a richer version of indigo – and that provides a good base, along with cerulean and a dab of indigo. A common error is to paint them a sort of lilac mauve as this is how we see them in our mind's eye, instead of using the plant itself as our guide and teacher.

Our little damson tree is by now nearing the end of its crop of fruit. Small but sweet, these are best cooked whole – so that the stones can separate from the flesh – and can then be used for winter sauces.

Bryony cascades up many of the trees and shrubs in our garden and the local hedgerows. The leaves have a most pleasing shape, vine like and usually symmetrical. Cut like a curvy maple leaf and combined with five-petalled, creamy green-veined flowers and the springy tendrils, the whole plant is a bonus. The fruits are green, orange and red, and are completely round and start matte in texture, becoming shiny and looking like a child's beads.

Alongside this, the elderberries glow dark purple violet and provide ample food for birds. The blackberries are still around and providing more food for wildlife and people alike, combining well with the surfeit of apples that we always have. Blackberry briars have usually escaped the hedgerow into the garden and so it is not necessary to wander far to gather a small basketful. This common plant is unusual in that it bears flowers and fruits at the same time. There are reputedly around 500 sub-species, and anyone who studies the genus Rubus is called a batologist.

Each autumn I am drawn again to Keble Martin, who has illustrated these plants so well, and a short walk along the track beside the garden takes us to an ancient thoroughfare that leads to a large plantation. The track has many species

Medlar and half

GLS
MMVI

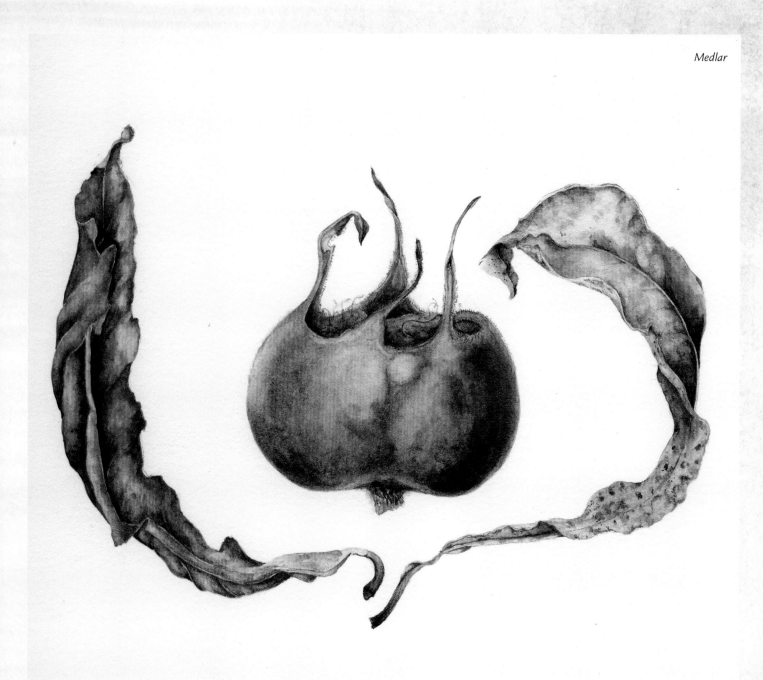

Medlar

Old Willow pattern cup and quinces

along its verges, and amongst them are many different brambles and other berries, the most special and tasty of which is, in my view, the dewberry. A blue fruit of large and few drupes that is fragrant and subtle in taste.

The track is called Pest House Lane, giving a clue as to the buildings, now long gone, that were farther along its length. Now it is part of the Hertfordshire Way. A favourite task is to forage for course material there, willow basket in hand. A few years ago I made such a trip and was trying to reach some wild plums high up in the hedgerow. I became aware of heavy breathing and a fellow being somewhere near. Conscious of being entirely alone and at least a mile from home, I wondered what situation I had got myself into. When I looked around I could see nothing but still hear the noise. When I concentrated on the direction of the noise I spotted a well-camouflaged fallow stag looking directly at me, head down, antlers up, about 25 yards away. After holding my breath and gazing at this beautiful animal, I slowly backed away and returned home, feeling richer and happier for my encounter.

Within the garden the medlars are the most amazing copper russet tones. With their metallic texture and long sepals they are most pleasing to draw and paint. Always a terminal fruit, they form lovely angles at the end of the stem. The flowers are large and reminiscent of a cross between a white dog rose and an apple blossom. Generous and tissue like, they unfold in May to lose their creases as they bask in the sun. Our small tree grows steadily and happily and fruits well, a favourite for the autumn workshop of 'autumn fruits' or 'painting jewel colours in autumn'. The preparation for this workshop is no hardship; a basket or two groan with the collected fruit of this and the neighbouring quince.

We have three quince trees. Only one of them bears fruit; the oldest and scrappiest of trees, it has lost its centre, and the gnarled and lichen-bearing branches seem too slight to bear these heavy fruits. Truly glowing, they are amber and green and yellow in one go. Mixing a single paint colour is futile; the fruit needs several colours overlaid in generous and wet washes to create its facsimile on paper.

Natural truth – Waining but still strong

Natural truth – Nearly spent

Natural truth – Magnolia grandiflora

NOVEMBER

It is my birthday in November, and I have always favoured this month above all others. A time when there is little pressure from the garden, save sweeping up fallen leaves, there is plenty to see and marvel over and paint. A gluttony of colour for sure. Leaves of every tone and hue appear as autumn continues and reaches her end.

The hedgerows are usually heavy with fruit; haws are alizarin with an under-wash of aureolin, providing a metallic appearance. They are full of vitamin C, and every year it is my intention to make hawthorn ketchup or jelly, but in the event they are left for the birds and another year's intention. Last rose hips hang from their thorny branches, bright red, in fact scarlet. Cutting one open you will see that, inside, these

Natural truth — Lunaria rediviva

Natural truth — Judith's lacecap

hairy seeds are surrounded by warm ochre orange flesh; and a wash of yellow under the scarlet of the skins will provide the best and most intense colour when painted.

While most of the prunus fruits have gone, the shepherd's bullace lasts well into November. These small fruits change from a glaucous green to a lovely soft apricot colour, and at dusk they hang and glow like hedgerow baubles in a way that gives me a bubble of excitement and comfort. By this time they are soft and sweet and can make a lovely bullace brandy that is most welcome on a winter evening.

The pear tree loses her leaves; and the pears, still pendulous, drop to the ground. Happily they feed many butterflies, and it is

Natural truth — Eriobotrya japonica

a great pleasure to watch for butterflies feeding before hibernation. The tortoiseshell and peacock seem especially to love the fallen pears, which only ripen after they fall from the tree.

We planted several varieties of crab apple over the last ten years, mostly for their fruit colour. There was already a huge mature tree with a leaning habit and dark bark, bronze foliage and deep cerise blossom followed by apples of a deep perylene violet or aubergine colour. Alongside this tree, standing in companionship, is another huge, old crab with apples that look like miniature bramleys, separated by a field maple. Nearby are Gorgeous, Sentinel, Rudolph, John Downie, Everest, Butterball and Golden Hornet, providing exciting colour in spring, summer and autumn. In autumn my favourites are Butterball and Golden Hornet, clinging on to illuminated fruit right through into winter.

Sloes now shine blackly or sing out a bright Prussian blue from the hedgerow depending on whether their bloom has been wiped off. They are best left until the first frosts for use in sloe gin or sloe vodka. The apples, including the prized russets, abound in our garden too – most of these trees date back to a time when

Bramley's seedling apple

the garden was much more important in feeding the household than it is today.

Cornus, honeysuckle and bryony add to the colours of hedgerow fruit – the dogwoods with their black fruit and red, black or apricot stems looking very smart – and are very useful in autumn compositions, looking regal in a jug of winter twigs for a painting workshop. The bryony is now every shade from green to yellow to orange to scarlet and all shades between. Often invisible when growing earlier in the seasons, they become very visible in late autumn when trees have lost their leaves and a bryony vine climbs high in the pear tree, twisting and turning, clad in berries like a Christmas garland.

Here and there peony seed heads are made of suede and are vibrant and rich golden browns, twisting this way and that. The leaves die back gradually and also twist and curl beautifully if you let them.

The grass has usually had its final cut by now but in the longer, wilder parts the dock and hogweed provide colour and texture. The dock is alizarin and carmine, and the last dock leaves are some of the most vibrantly coloured leaves you will find anywhere.

So you can see that, while the light

Tortoiseshell and pear

fades as autumn changes to winter, there is still in fact much colour to find in the garden, the hedgerow and the verges. For the painter a plus of these subjects is that they are less prone to change and shape-shifting. They are not opening, moving, seeking the light, petals twisting; they are slow and contemplative and sit willingly to be drawn and painted.

The last hydrangeas brought in twist and turn and dry to glorious colours not usually found in flowers: metallic blues and lilacs, verdigris greens and turquoises.

November is a month when we usually go away. Teaching has concluded for the year, and remoter shores beckon. I travel with my paints and always try and paint what I find locally. Typically this will involve a remote cottage in the Scottish Highlands. Recently these seem to be right on the shorelines; and seaweeds wash up in the most lovely shades of yellow green, ochre and rust.

And so, as the days draw shorter and the air is more laden with frost, the final leaves of autumn flutter their reds and ochres to the ground as if signalling the close of the season. The first proper frosts give an icy thrill as winter beckons and the garden, the verge and hedgerow, together with the painter, prepare for winter as once again we are all too aware of 'The Measure of the Year'.

Heracleum in winter coat

Hydrangea – dear Ayesha

Hydrangea — the pale blue hydrangea

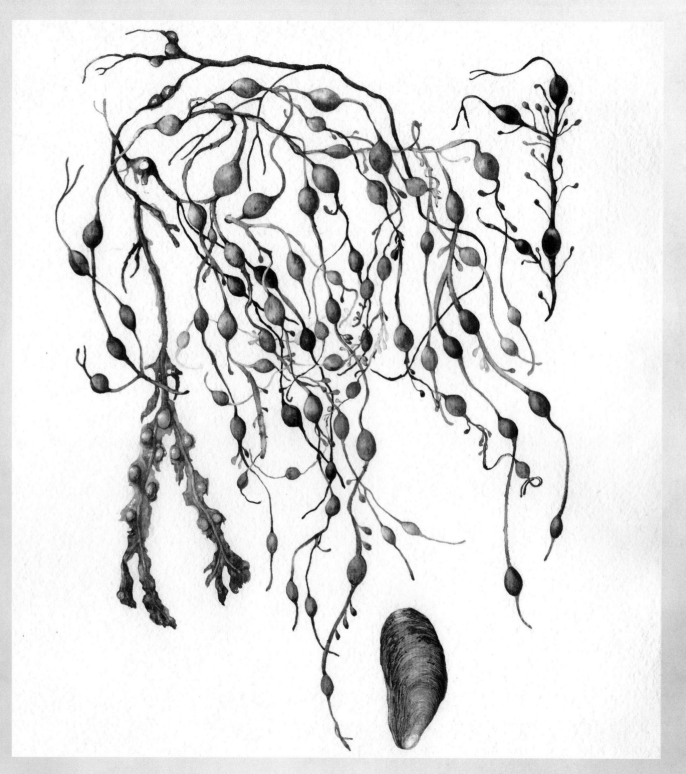

The seahorse

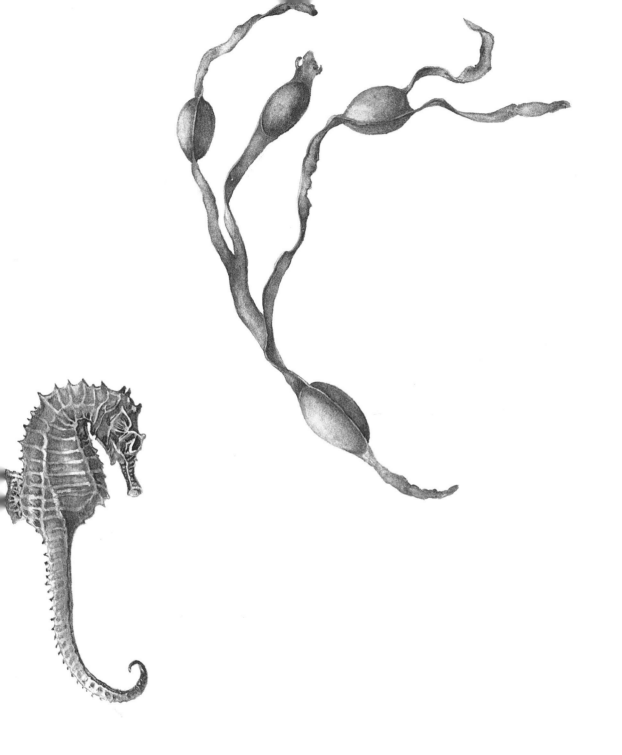

BOTANICAL PAINTING: AN OVERVIEW

INTRODUCTION

Botanical painting and illustration are based on a set of techniques to achieve an accurate and usually life-size plant portrait. They have developed from the traditions of showing a plant on paper or vellum so that the subject could be identified. Botanical illustration dates back many hundreds of years when plants were painted in illuminations. Plants were also used in the monasteries for health and healing; correct identification could be critical to survival.

In the last 400 years, illustration has developed to identify plants with medicinal attributes as well as those with chemical and manufacturing properties. Before photography it was important to capture the plant's likeness accurately. Some of the early botanical artists were producing precise high-quality work with limited colour palettes and often in poor lighting conditions.

The Dutch Masters painted a range of flowers of different seasons, often in the same arrangement, indicating the wealth of the commissioner and carrying messages about longevity, love and wealth. Similarly, over the last thousand years plants and flowers have been used in tapestry, embroidery, paintings and fabrics to decorative effect.

Even since the advent of photography, painting is still used to illustrate plants for identification purposes. Most modern plant identification books, especially of a specific plant type (a monograph) or of wild flowers, still use illustrations.

Most botanical gardens employ artists or illustrators who often use the herbarium specimens collected abroad to develop illustrations back home. There are large collections of botanical works in the Fitzwilliam Museum, Cambridge; and in the Lindley Library and at the Natural History Museum, both in London.

Materials and equipment

See table above. When taking the plunge and attempting botanical drawing and painting, use the best materials and equipment that you can afford. If you have a limited budget, then buy a more restricted range of colours, use a plain white china plate as a palette, and buy mixed-hair brushes. Use your 'best' paper carefully, and test colours on lesser stock.

Planning your work; studying and understanding the plant

Spend time studying the plant. You do need to understand the structure, its colours and textures before you can begin to draw. If you can, use more than one

Paper	Usually hot pressed (very smooth) watercolour paper. Fabriano, Canson or Arches all perform well. The paper we use is made of cotton or linen rag or a combination and is pressed smooth through hot rollers and sized with gelatine to aid clean edges to the work and flow of the paint on the paper.
Pencils	HB, 2B and 2H (or at least an HB)
Sharpener	A good sharpener that will give your pencils a good point
Eraser	A softish eraser, or a kneadable putty rubber
Dividers	...or a pair of school compasses for measured drawings
Paints	Watercolour paints (usually half pans). The following colours are useful: indigo, French ultramarine, cobalt blue, sap green, aureolin, lemon yellow, permanent mauve, Winsor violet, scarlet lake, permanent rose (these colours are Winsor & Newton)
Brushes	Good quality brushes are critical for this art form, but can be very expensive. Rosemary & Co brushes are very good value as are Da Vinci, in 0, 1, 2, 3, or Winsor & Newton series 7 sable brushes, in 00, 0, 1, 2, 3
Palette	Ideally a china palette or a white plate or tile
Board	A drawing board, or very stiff cardboard, also a small cushion or book to lean the board on and give a slight tilt to the board
Others	Tracing paper, cartridge paper, kitchen roll

specimen and cut one open, looking at the elements that contribute to the form, size, shape and colours. If you get these wrong in your drawing then the final painting will not be convincing. Consider carefully the colours – are they heavy, dark, light, soft? How might you convey this with your paints? Use a light source from the side opposite your preferred hand – ie, from the left if you are right-handed. This might be a window (try and avoid direct sunlight) or a lamp. Also ensure that where you are working is clean and dry.

What layout are you going to use? A couple of leaves or even petals can make a very attractive study on the page. Think about what you want to convey when you select your plant material: do you want to paint a traditional portrait or do you want to attempt a more artistic picture – what is the purpose behind your work? Look at layouts of other work you have seen – what do you like and why? What is going on with the balance of the work? Ensure that heavy flowers have an adequate stem to balance them – try and avoid putting a very straight stem in the middle of the paper.

Think about working with a border or mount so that you can consider your layout from the start. Remember that odd numbers tend to work better than even. Three of something placed can work well. Alternatively, designs with curves can succeed in leading the eye around the composition.

Drawing

You may wish to draw on to a separate piece of paper and then trace off on to your finished piece. This can allow for changed placement on the page – but it is time consuming. Use a medium pencil such as an HB for drawing, and do not press too hard. If you need to rub out and you have pressed hard, then there will be indentations left on the paper.

You can make a sketchy drawing if this is how you work best and then define the detail of edges later, before painting. If your hand is not flowing, try to draw from your shoulder, sweeping the pencil on the paper. Try to loosen up and relax if you get stiff. Consider the overall shape of a flower. If you are struggling then get the basic shape right. Is it a cup, a saucer, a tube or a mix of those? The idea is to have a light line drawing that you are going to colour. The holly (right) is a practice to try and work out colour and painting method.

Preparing to paint: studying the plant

Look at the plant and consider the light and dark. As well as using accurate colour you need to consider where there is shadow. Is there reflected light and what colour is this? For example, on a shiny holly leaf it may be pale blue; on a more matte leaf it may be a sheen of pale blue. Sit back from the plant and really study it. Where are there highlights and where are the darkest parts? Use photographs if necessary to help you to think about light

Variegated holly study sheet

and dark. Remember this is about creating an illusion of form on the paper to show the structure and shape of the plant.

Getting the colour right

Consider what colours, either pure or mixed, will create the right impression. Keep a note of what you use so that you can refer back to it later, or when you need to mix more colour. If possible, use pure colour as mixing can create dullness. Some colours are very hard to achieve, such as some pinks and purples – eg, geraniums – and you may need to buy the exact colour. Some paints are prefixed by the words

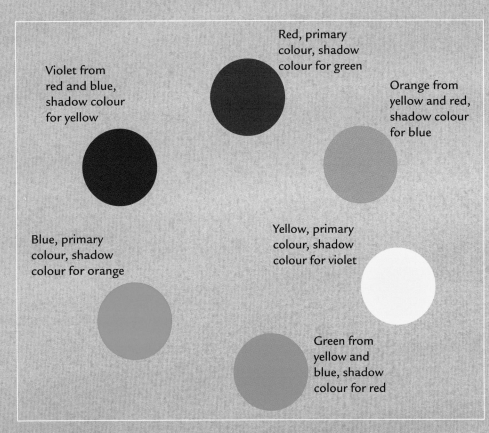

Violet from red and blue, shadow colour for yellow

Red, primary colour, shadow colour for green

Orange from yellow and red, shadow colour for blue

Blue, primary colour, shadow colour for orange

Yellow, primary colour, shadow colour for violet

Green from yellow and blue, shadow colour for red

'brilliant' or 'bright', and they do seem to have a glowing quality on the paper.

Be very careful when mixing greens; consider the leaf or stem texture that you want to achieve. Use a practice piece before you commit colour to your work. Check whether the paint you are using is transparent or opaque, and practise first to see the effect of the paint on paper and the paint laid over other colours.

If you are not used to mixing colours then you may wish to complete colour lines, mixing a yellow and a blue, starting with one colour and mixing a small quantity of the other colour, increasing each time and laying these out as a line of paint samples. Note the paints you use, and these can form an interesting reference tool.

Painting – shadow or colour first?

Some people prefer to paint all the shadow first and then use the colour as a series of layers or glazes over the top.

This can work well for some pale and for some bright flowers where the colours can be 'muddied' or dulled by the later application of shadow. Other people prefer to build up layers of washes first, using the paper to create light and dark, allowing the deeper colour to define form and then only painting shadow towards the end. Most people use a combination of methods to achieve the effect they want.

There is a convention, which some people use, that the colour of the shadow is the complementary colour to the colour of the flower or leaf (see colour wheel, left). So, a red flower will have a green shadow, a blue flower an orange shadow, etc. This sounds improbable, but does seem to work. For best results practise before applying to your work.

Probably for best results, a grey of transparent yellow, ultramarine and alizarin can be mixed with a bias towards the complementary colour. For example, if using this for a yellow flower, mix more red and blue so that the grey has a violet hue. This usually helps the shadow mix to look harmonious. For best effect test the colour you might use: does it look natural?

Laying down washes

Washes of watercolour can be built up to give depth of colour, and this gives an indication of form or shape. Remember not to paint over highlights (this is where the light hits something, making it look very light or shiny), and for the lightest parts leave the white of the paper showing. This is especially important for shine, such as on a holly leaf. You can build up washes and fade away to white. This can be achieved with two brushes, one with paint and the other with water. This allows quick blending. It can be useful to practise to prevent hard edges, 'cauliflowers' and buckling. Ensure the paint is dry before applying the next layer.

Practise the effect of mixing paints in the palette and on to your paper as follows:

Palette mixing
Mix a transparent red and a transparent blue in your palette. Paint on to your paper and look at the effect. For reference, paint the two separate colours and label them on your practice piece.

Mixing on the paper
This is a wet into wet (well, really, it's damp into damp to prevent puddling) technique. You may wish to dampen the paper and allow it to dry to a slight sheen (not shiny as this is too wet). Place one of your colours on to the paper and blend with the dampness of the paper. Rinse your brush and pick up the other colour, blending this with the first colour, straight on the paper. This can be ideal for achieving mottled effects as where two colours meet in nature they are rarely neat and tidy – for example, colour changes on the skin of a plum. This does require practice to learn

Commissioned heart in progress I

how to use the right amount of paint.

Optical mix – or overlaying washes
This technique can work well to build up some textures – for example, blooms on fruit or where colours appear to be built up in the petal, such as in some irises or rose petals. Paint a clear wash of one colour and allow it to dry completely. Place another colour over the top – again allow

to dry. This technique can also be used to achieve velvety textures, for example on pansy petals.

Dry brush work and detail
Having built up shadow and colour you will reach a point where you need to use a 'dry' brush to put in more detail. The brush is not really dry, but damp, and

this gives greater control of the paint.

You are no longer creating washes, but instead almost drawing with the brush and putting in detail that describes the plant to others. This might include more shadow and darks to define further the form or shape of your subject, markings, stamens, hairs, etc. When you think you have finished, stand back from the work and really consider what is going on with it – is the balance right, is there sufficient shadow? If you are struggling, hold the work up to a mirror: it can help you to see the 'whole' painting.

It is very hard to appraise your work critically when you have been leaning over it slavishly for hours. Often we seem to see only the little bits of paint and not a coherent whole. Stand away from your work – leave it and look at it later. Some people leave their work out on their easel and walk past it, observing critically. What is going on in the painting – is there colour balance? Look at your painting from different distances – the subject should be clear, balanced and identifiable from any distance.

When you have critically appraised your work, go back and correct or add to your painting. This might involve more detail, but for most of us it is a combination of depth of tone and shadow and balance between leaf and flower.

You may want to put your work away and get it out in a few weeks and appraise it again – it is hard to be pleased or critical sometimes.

Naming, signing and mounting your work
Make sure naming and signing fit with the overall impression you have sought to create. Do you want to use a logo, initials, etc? Do you want to use the correct name for the plant? Consider a mount and frame that do not detract or distract from your painting. Finally, enjoy and feel proud!

PAINTING ON VELLUM

Narcissus and the pheasant feather

Much of my work within this book is painted on vellum, which I source from William Cowley of Newport Pagnell. This is a place I have visited on many occasions and where we made the *BBC Countryfile* programme in which I was featured painting on vellum.

Vellum is calfskin, and almost all that we use today is a by-product of the meat industry. Sadly, much of this part of the animal would find its way into landfill if it were not taken by William Cowley to be processed using age-old techniques into vellum that can be used by artists and calligraphers of today.

Until recently, all the statutes of Her Majesty's Government were written on to skins produced at William Cowley. Books of importance were written on to animal skins going back thousands of years. Legal documents were written on parchment as the ink (usually made from oak galls) became indelible, meaning the document could not be altered without it being apparent. Their durability means that they are still here for us to see today: documents such as indentures, wills and illuminations.

I paint on vellum because of the results it produces. The paint sits on the surface of the material, and as layers are meticulously built up it produces a luminous quality in the paint; the colours rich and vibrant. It is not a surface that takes washes, and a drier approach is required or the brush can suddenly remove layers that have been built up over hours. I love the fact that this skin has experienced life, has hopefully been well treated and respected, and then processed with skill and attention to detail before I get to work on it.

Preparing the vellum

Some artists prepare their vellum by gluing it on to board. The glue used is a natural substance made from boiled-up pieces of cut vellum (like rabbit skin glue) or flour and water paste. If this approach is used it is best to take guidance from the supplier in respect of the specific type of vellum that you have and to follow the instructions in a calligraphy or illumination instruction book.

Most vellum that is purchased from Cowley is ready prepared for painting. Some is slightly cockled; and, remembering that vellum is a natural skin, it will respond to atmospheric changes and will curl in damp or hot conditions.

For this reason, keep vellum dry and out of damp or humid or excessively dry conditions where there will be fluctuations in temperature or humidity.

Whether using 'Manuscript' or 'Kelmscott' vellum, the surface is very slick and can often benefit from a rubbing of pounce or pumice powder, although it is considered ready for use. Pounce is a mix of talc and pumice (usually) and finely 'sands' the surface, helping watercolour paints to 'key' on to the surface. Do not ingest this powder. If the surface is too slick or greasy the paint will sometimes move into small 'bubbles' or puddles of paint, similar to when painting on to china, and it can be difficult to build up even layers of colour.

Manuscript and natural calfskin vellum are less flat and thick than Kelmscott but can have more 'bite' for the paint. Look at the vellum under a magnifier as you will need to use what was the hairy side of the skin. The other side had the fat against it and usually is more greasy and slick than the hair side.

Drawing

Ideally do not draw directly on to the vellum. Draw on to hot pressed or cartridge paper and then trace off on to the vellum. If you do draw directly then draw on to vellum with a hardish pencil (H or 2H) as the graphite seems to work more softly than the lead hardness would suggest. Keep pencil lines light and minimal.

Rubbing out

Vellum is reasonably resilient and will permit gentle rubbing out, although be careful here as some erasers seem to transfer a grease that resists the paint. Similarly, any graphite smudges can usually be lifted, but it is better to dab gently rather than rub vigorously at the vellum. An alternative is to use pounce to rub off pencil lines.

Watch points!

Keep hands away from your face or neck when working on vellum as this is a good way to transfer grease and oils which make it hard to use.

Use transparent colours when you paint, for glowing effect; and remember that opaque colours tend to look much more matte than on paper as the paints really sit on the surface of the vellum. This means that you need to be more aware than usual of the qualities and properties of your paints.

If you find that an area is not taking paint well, then leave it to dry and gently rub a little pounce with the tip of your little finger on that area. It will remove some of your work but should make it easier for successive layers of paint to adhere to the surface.

Painting on vellum

Some people take to vellum more than others – for some it is a delight to work on, and for others it is sheer hell! I find that people who are quite dry painters will often work more happily with it than wetter painters – but this is not always so.

Keep a test piece of the same quality as you are using so that you can test colours and how the paint is handling. Also use this piece if you need to lift any paint – have a practice and see how this piece of vellum 'behaves'.

Some artists do use washes; it is best to use thin, transparent washes and to leave them to dry thoroughly before adding the next layer – longer than one might on watercolour paper. Graded washes work to some extent, but blended washes tend not to be successful. This is because vellum is not as absorbent as paper, and the paint sits on the vellum.

Some artists use small brush marks, almost stippling with the paint, and build up depth of colour this way (eg, Marie Angel). Others use cross-hatching, and some paint with a more or less dry brush as they might on paper. It is best to develop one's own technique to suit preferred style and also subject matter.

Washes on vellum can be used on small areas, but the best technique is a fairly dry brush. Be careful not to use colours too thickly, and for best effect use transparent colours or small amounts of opaque colours, remembering that the latter will sit on the surface over other colours, often masking them.

If you make a mistake, use water and paper towel to lift off. Much of your work can be lifted, so if you do correct make sure you are happy to lift off, rather than just wanting to lighten an area, as you might on paper. If you do lift a large area of paint then you will need to allow it to dry thoroughly and you can then rub some pounce on to the vellum to make the surface more matte if it has become at all slick or greasy. You can also lift using a curved scalpel blade (and extreme care!) and scrape off your error.

Use spotter brushes which give good control and reasonable paint holding as you will not use many wash techniques. Using a small brush, extremely clean edges and lines can be accomplished, and as the paint does not bleed into the fibres (as it does on paper) exquisite detail can be achieved. To finish off go into shadow areas, consider whether any of the work needs uniting with a slight 'wash' – or more of a 'damp', if such existed! (being careful of opaque or chalky colours which tend to 'lift'). Stand back and watch your work glow.

Painting on vellum – steps
● *Select a subject that is simple and will not require large areas of washes as vellum does not take washes very readily, or unless you have a lot of experience of painting on vellum*
● *With masking tape, tape your piece of vellum to a piece of paper on which you can test colours*
● *On another piece of paper, draw the subject*
● *Trace off with tracing paper, use an HB pencil*

Iris cimarron strip

on the back of the tracing paper and transfer
with a sharp 2H pencil to achieve a fine graphite
line on the vellum

● *Mix paints, trying to keep to transparent colours*

● *Paint any first washes carefully, keeping*
within the lines, and allow to dry for longer than
you would paper

● *Develop form with small brush strokes on the*
vellum, being careful not to lift the paint that
you have already placed on it

● *Again, give plenty of time to dry between*
applications of paint

● *Complete and enjoy!*

Mounting vellum

Vellum needs slightly careful treatment
when mounting. Use acid-free paper
conservation tape. Place the vellum face
down on a clean surface. Secure two
vertical strips of tape to the top of the
vellum using a horizontal strip. With the
two vertical strips as 'hinges', hang the
vellum from the mount – attaching it to
the back of the mount. This allows the
vellum full freedom. Then 'sandwich' the
vellum between the mount and a piece of
mount board backing that is larger than
the piece of vellum. Stick the backing
board to the mount. This leaves the
vellum free but contained and safe. For
storage, use acid-free tissue paper – or
frame as any other surface.

Supplier

William Cowley, Parchment Works,
97 Caldecote Street, Newport Pagnell,
Buckinghamshire MK16 0DB (tel:
01908 610038).

Further reading

Painting for Calligraphers by Marie Angel
(Overlook Press, 1984).
Vellum Preparation: History and Technique by
Paul T Werner (Orange Press, 2002).

LEFT Palimpsest yellow beetle; BELOW Lantern bug

RIGHT Palimpsest blue beetle; BELOW Jewel beetle

ACKNOWLEDGEMENTS

The following people and institutions have influenced or informed my work:

Christabel King, one of Kew's finest botanical artists. I started an evening class in botanical illustration at Capel Manor College around 1990 with Christabel; she suggested I exhibit with the RHS when I was still in my twenties. It took me another couple of decades to do this.

Madingley Hall, University of Cambridge, where I have worked many times with Valerie Oxley, Judith Pumphrey and my dearest friend Carole Astbury.

Helga Hislop (*www.wildlybotanical.co.uk*) has been a mentor extraordinaire. She likes to see all I produce on vellum, and I hope I have been a worthy protégé. Thank you, Helga.

Artists who continue to inspire me are Rosie Sanders (*www.rosiesanders.com*), my friend and Society of Botanical Artists co-conspirator Billy Showell (*www.billyshowell.com*) and the late Rory McEwen. McEwen was an extraordinary artist, and early on I made it my mission to research his meticulous work. Most of his work was on vellum, and this no doubt influenced my choice of this surface.

The Royal Horticultural Society (*http://staging.rhs.org.uk/education-learning/libraries-at-rhs/articles/from-petal-to-pigment*) and the Hunt Institute of Botanical Documentation (*www.huntbotanical.org*) have provided opportunities to seize and in which to excel.

Having artwork in both the Hunt and the RHS Lindley Library and an RHS gold medal are amongst my best achievements.

The BBC has filmed me twice for programmes, and these short films help to punctuate one's career, offering consolidation and validation as well as a valuable opportunity to see oneself as through the eyes of others.

Tools of my trade include: Fabriano and Canson papers; Schmincke, Holbein, Daniel Smith and Old Holland paints; Raphael and da Vinci brushes; and, perhaps most importantly, vellum from Paul Wright of William Cowley (*www.williamcowley.co.uk*). For those with specific ethical concerns, vellum is today a by-product of the meat industry. Without its production, animal skins would be discarded.

Cambridge University Botanic Garden (*www.botanic.cam.ac.uk*) has been a backdrop where I have felt part of the team for more than 10 years. To be in Darwin's garden is indeed a privilege. Field Breaks (*www.fieldbreaks.co.uk*) has afforded me similar opportunities (thank you, Sue), and there is something very pleasing about sitting with a group discussing the finer points of shadows or colour mixes.

I have been a member of the Society of Botanical Artists (*www.soc-botanical-artists.org*) for more than a decade, and am now Vice President and on the picture selection committee; I feel proud to promote and be involved in

the world of contemporary botanical art.

Rosy Naylor (*www.platformdesign.co.uk*) has worked with me for many years to develop my websites where you can see more of my work (*www.gaelsellwood.co.uk* and *www.paint-nature.co.uk*).

Bob and Gary of PhotoartGB (*www.photoartgb.com*) have scanned all the work for inclusion in this book, often helping to turn around a job superfast. Thank you both so much.

Rachel Warne (*www.rachelwarne.co.uk*) has photographed me at work and in the garden, and has produced the photographs herein which describe the garden and studio perfectly. Thank you, Rachel.

Alan and Marion Marshall of Mascot Media (*www.mascotmedia.co.uk*) have offered guidance and a helping hand to me as author; above all, they have shown confidence in me, my writing and artwork, and I am pleased to be a part of their stable of artists. Thank you both.

Finally, I wish to acknowledge the encouragement of my parents. I was expected to achieve, to be the best, to aim for greatness and to be my own teacher and critic in my chosen field. It has mostly stood me in good stead and, above all, has made me an independent and determined perfectionist. As we say in our family: "I didn't get where I am today", although it feels as though perhaps I have, and whether it is in the garden or the studio it feels quite good…